Living in Grace

A 30-Day Devotional

Living in Grace

A 30-Day Devotional

REDLAND BAPTIST CHURCH

Living in Grace: A 30-Day Devotional

For publishing information, visit GoodCommaEditing.com.

ISBN: 978-1-964895-05-5

Table of Contents

REDLAND
BAPTIST CHURCH

a grace-driven people
for a grace-needing world

Connecting the heart
of Montgomery County
with the heart of Christ

where people
Grow in the love of Christ
Reach in the name of Christ
Affirm in the body of Christ
Care in the nature of Christ
Exalt in the glory of Christ

A Brief History of Redland

Redland Baptist Church began in 1966 with twenty-one people meeting at a member's home. Over the years, many more have joined this fellowship, and our church has expanded in both physical size and spiritual impact through community programs and church planting. Now, hundreds of people gather each week on our thirteen-acre campus in the Derwood area of Montgomery County, Maryland, a suburb of Washington, DC.

Hi, friend,

It brings me joy to know that you are holding this devotional book in your hands. Inside this book, you will find encouragement from thirty different members of the Redland Baptist Church family. These members represent many different ages, experiences, and walks of life, but all of them have found in Redland a place they can call home.

So many of us love Redland because God has enabled us to build deep relationships, grow in mature faith, express our gifts in ministry, and receive care during times of need. My prayer is that if you do not already have a church family, you too will experience the same connection that we have here.

I have known the joy of serving at Redland since 2009. My closest relationships have been built here. With these wonderful people, I have laughed until I cried and cried until I was ready to laugh again. I have prayed fervently with them and have seen some incredible answers to prayer. I have stood with them while worshiping the Lord as we sensed His awesome presence together. I have labored with them in joyful ministry. This is a true family. As with any family, there have been occasional bumps. On those occasions, I have seen humility and forgiveness on display.

You can tell that I am biased about this church! But what makes Redland so wonderful is that all the goodness that flows through this church body can be attributed only to Jesus Christ. Our foundation is Jesus our Savior, who died for our sins and rose again. We love to study His Word, the Bible, and apply it to our lives. All the special things that I love about Redland are simply a reflection of our amazing God who is at work here.

You may be holding this devotional book because you visited our church, or perhaps a friend gave the book to you. Whether you are looking for a church home or are just passing through, my prayer is that the devotionals in this short volume will contribute to your spiritual growth.

Spending devotional time with God may be a familiar practice for you, or it may be a new experience. These devotional readings are designed so that you can complete one each day for a month. If you miss a day, do not worry; just pick it up again the next day. Each devotional reading can be completed in about ten minutes, but you may enjoy taking a little more time for contemplation and prayer. You may try working through each devotional like this:

Pray. Ask God to help you see what He wants you to see before you begin.

Read the passage. Read the Bible passage listed, using a translation or version you find most helpful. Consider what the passage means and note any questions you have.

Read the devotional. Note the key verse at the top, which helps set the tone. Then, read the devotional piece. You will find a personal account from each writer with an explanation of how his or her experience relates to the Bible passage.

Pray. If you need help responding to the devotional with prayer, a short prayer prompt is provided to help you get started. You can pray for as long or as short as you like.

Consider. You may wish to reread the Bible passage after the devotional text. Then, read the questions and answer them. If you partner with another person to read this devotional, this portion is perfect for providing topics of discussion.

As you seek God's face, I believe firmly that He will bless your efforts. If you find a certain devotional to be meaningful, consider reaching out to the one who wrote it to share how it blessed you. I am sure that person would be encouraged by your words!

If you and I have not connected yet, I sincerely hope we do soon. May the Lord bless you as you read.

In Christ,

Kevin Freeman
Acting Pastor

God Sees

– DAY 1 –

Enjoy the Goodness Seen in God's Creation

"God saw all that He had made, and it was very good." (Genesis 1:31)

Have you seen any insects today? I spotted a fly whizzing around the back porch. Later, I spied a butterfly fluttering around the flowers in our garden. Then, in the evening, I watched fireflies flickering over the lawn. Perhaps you, like me, have wondered why God created certain less-appealing insects, like mosquitoes, wasps, and cockroaches. But even insects we think of as "pests" are part of God's creation. Insects maintain a balanced ecosystem, improve agriculture, provide food, and, most importantly, accomplish God's purpose. All living things have value because God created them, and all creation brings glory to the Creator. I care about insects because God cares about insects.

The beautiful poetry of Genesis 1 tells us God made the world and everything in it. God gives all mankind life, breath, and every ability. God, the Thinker, planned it; God, the Engineer, built it; God, the Artist, made it beautiful; and God, the Father, made it our home. At the end of each day of creation, God pronounced it "good."

In the heavens, God fine-tunes dozens of parameters within narrow ranges in order for life of any kind to exist. Underground, God commands earthworms to till the soil and distribute nutrients to balance the ecosystem. Within each of us, God places a brain that uses incredibly sophisticated neural processing systems, designed perfectly for us to interact with our environment. We are fearfully and wonderfully made. The universe, the earth, and the people inhabiting the earth are all designed by the Creator to work together in harmony, like a choir singing praise and glory to God. And God called this "very good." All creation is "very good" for the purposes for which it was designed.

We can look at the stars in the night sky and see in them the glory of God. We can look upon the trees and the growing crops and think about the gracious provision of God. We can look upon the blooming flowers and breathe the fragrance of God's purity and beauty. All creation sings praise to the Creator. We can learn its language and hearken to its truth.

Lord, help me to receive the beauty and richness of nature as a gift from You. Out of nothing, You have made everything, and, for that, a song of praise is due. Glory! Glory! Glory! Glory to You, our Lord!

– Reflect –

Read Genesis 1:26–31.

1. What amazes you most about God's creation? How does this draw you to consider God's goodness?

2. What aspect of God's creation can you thank Him for today that you might typically take for granted?

About the Author

Tom Garin spent his early years in New York City. In 2016, he and his wife, Lois, became members of Redland Baptist Church, where they enjoy serving as deacons. One of Tom's passions is learning about God and creation from Christian scientists at the Discovery Institute.

– DAY 2 –

See Yourself as God Sees You

"Your eyes saw my unformed body; all the days ordained for me were written in your book before one of them came to be." (Psalm 139:16)

I needed to leave for my brother's retirement ceremony but still could not decide what to wear. As I hurriedly sifted through the clothes in my closet, I spotted a dress that seemed appropriate, although I had not worn it in a very long time. It was nearing the time to leave, so I quickly put on the dress, grabbed my coffee mug, and ran out the door. When I got to my car, I noticed a stain on my dress. Unfortunately, it was too late to run back in and find something different to put on, so I went to the ceremony with the stained dress.

Despite feeling self-conscious about the stain, I realized at the end of the ceremony that no one in my family had said anything about it. My mom had even complimented me on how nice I looked. Because she is my mom and would lovingly compliment me regardless of how I looked, I figured that she surely had seen the stain and was kindly ignoring it. However, when I asked her if she had seen it, she told me that she never would have noticed it had I not pointed it out to her.

We often see only our stains, our perceived shortcomings. We wear stains of inadequacy, failure, and past regrets. These stains tell us that we will never measure up to the expectations of others. We convince ourselves that our stains are our defining feature. God sees us differently. Psalm 139 explains that God saw you and me before we were born. He uniquely fashioned each of us before we first drew breath. We have each been given a name, a purpose, and a mission. Despite knowing our stains, God looks past them to our heart. We need not second-guess how He created us. What we view as stains often become God's means to empower us and work through us to help others.

God does not see the stains. He sees His creation, His child, His beloved. If you are in Christ Jesus, He sees you as spotless. If God sees us in such a positive light, should we not also value ourselves as individual and unique creatures?

Lord, remove any incorrect perceptions I have about myself. Help me to go forward in freedom, loving and seeing myself and others the way You do.

– Reflect –

Read Psalm 139:13–18.

1. How might God's view of your perceived shortcomings differ from your perspective?

2. Do you believe you have a purpose? How do you know?

About the Author

Jen Saunders was a college minister for nineteen years before coming to Redland, where she serves as interim children's ministry director. Jen loves spending time with her church family and with her family in upstate New York (where she grew up). She also enjoys journaling, catching up with friends, and being with her dog, Gracie.

– DAY 3 –

Cultivate a Heart That God Delights to See

"But the Lord said to Samuel, 'Do not consider his appearance or his height, for I have rejected him. The Lord does not look at the things people look at. People look at the outward appearance, but the Lord looks at the heart.'"
(1 Samuel 16:7)

We live in a status-centered world, do we not? The richer people are, or the more attractive they are, the more they seem to be loved and adored by society. These superficial factors are often treated as more important than a person's deeper qualities. It does not matter how callous, self-centered, or even malevolent a person may be. Outward appearances often hold great sway in this world.

To gain recognition in such an externally focused culture, we often find ourselves searching for outward indicators of status. These may include the car we drive, the clothing we wear, or the place we live. We may strive to keep up with the latest trends and fads to remain accepted by others. Is this the sort of status we should be seeking? Our efforts may get us into the desired social circles here on earth, but it would be wiser instead for us to concentrate our efforts on how we measure up in the eyes of God.

When choosing the next king of Israel, God was not seeking a man who was revered in the eyes of others—someone physically impressive, charming, or well-spoken. That sort of superficial status did not matter to Him. Rather, God was seeking what mattered most: the condition of the heart. The heart is a reflection of a person's true nature. God is not interested in outward appearances, those personas that people often alter to suit the preferences of others. Instead, God looks for hearts that are good, clean, true, and without pretense. God sees through our "make-believe" personas and judges us accordingly. Though others may be easily swayed by haughty, smooth talkers, God is not fooled. He did not find anything suitable in David's brothers that qualified them to lead His people, because God was looking beyond the outward appearance.

Though many people blindly chase whatever is flashy or appealing to the flesh, God calls us to pursue deeper, more lasting qualities. While we can never truly measure up to God's standard on our own, let us call upon the Holy Spirit to cultivate in us hearts that please God—hearts that are clean in God's sight and focused on serving others rather than ourselves.

Day 3

God, give me a clean and true heart so that I may follow You. Shape my desires to reflect Yours so that I can be used by You. Help me to focus on the qualities that You value.

– Reflect –

Read 1 Samuel 16:6–13.

1. What aspects of your character reflect a heart that pleases God? In what ways do you fall short?

2. In the past week, what actions have you taken that indicate you are cultivating a heart that is pleasing to God?

About the Author

Marilyn Jordan grew up in Oklahoma and moved to Maryland in 1976. She joined Redland Baptist Church in 1981 and has faithfully served as the church pianist for over thirty-six years. She and her husband, Paul, have three children and three grandchildren, all of whom were either dedicated to Christ or baptized at Redland.

– DAY 4 –

Hope in God, Who Watches Over You

"The Lord will watch over your coming and going both now and forevermore." (Psalm 121:8)

Growing up, the unknown always frightened me. When I was seven, my family bought a new house. On our last day in our old house, I ran to my empty closet to hide, seeking solace in a place I found comfortable and familiar. As I have gotten older, I have experienced other changes, from beginning a new school to starting a new job. Each of my experiences has been uniquely difficult. But I have learned to look for help not in what seems comfortable and familiar but in Christ alone.

My growing understanding of God's steadfast hand in my life brought me comfort when I was preparing to embark on what was then the biggest change of my life: moving seven hours away from my family to attend college. Although the new opportunity thrilled me, I was apprehensive about the challenges I would face without my family by my side. This new endeavor spurred me toward deeper trust in the Lord.

In Psalm 121, the psalmist faces a physical journey filled with challenges and unknown circumstances, too. Every year, the Israelites would make a journey to Jerusalem for the three religious pilgrimage festivals of the Jewish calendar year. This journey was over hills and through scorching deserts. As the psalmist started this journey, his first, natural instinct was fear. The traveler searched for help around and within himself, but only by looking up to heaven did he realize that all help comes from the Lord.

Understanding that his help came from the Creator of the hills and scorching deserts gave the psalmist hope for the journey. In verses 3 and 4, we find that God knows us and will never stop watching over us. Verses 5 and 6 describe God's protection over His followers. The final two verses remind us that the Lord is preserving us for our future eternity with Him.

As Christians, we can use this literal journey of the Israelites to reflect on our faith journey. When we are overwhelmed about the road ahead, it is important we seek help from the one "who made heaven and earth."

Dear heavenly Father, I praise You because You have made heaven and earth and still care about me. Thank You for always being my help. As I continue my faith journey, I pray that You will remind me that You know me, You will protect me, and You are constantly with me. Please guide me to share this gift of help with everyone I meet.

– Reflect –

Read Psalm 121.

1. What challenges lead you to become distressed? Why? To what or whom do you turn for help in times of anxiety?

2. Which promise from verses 3–8 do you find to be the most comforting? Why?

About the Author

Jillian Holmes is an accounting student at Cedarville University. When she is not studying, you are most likely to find Jillian on a paddle board or enjoying God's splendor at a national park.

– DAY 5 –

Let God Lead You

"I am with you and will watch over you wherever you go, and I will bring you back to this land. I will not leave you until I have done what I have promised you." (Genesis 28:15)

Sometimes we seek God only when we are in crisis, or perhaps we seek Him only after finding ourselves on the backside of bad choices we have made. Or maybe we know very little about God and are not used to seeking Him.

As a child, I knew about seeking God only in crisis situations. I suppose I viewed Him as "the God for when things got tough." There was no need, I assumed, to trouble such a God for daily living. While I knew how to make an "emergency call" to God, I really did not know who was on the other end of line. I saw Him as a God for my family needs but not yet the God of my life.

The Old Testament patriarchs, Abraham, Isaac, and Jacob, are some of the most foundational people in the Jewish and Christian faiths. Though Jacob had been raised in the house of Isaac, God seemed to be only his family's God—the God of his father and grandfather. The Bible gives no indication that Jacob had a personal relationship with God until he was in a crisis.

Today's devotional passage finds Jacob on the run from a life-threatening family dispute. Jacob's brother, Esau, had intentions of killing him because Jacob had once again taken something precious from him. Once Jacob's deviousness was exposed, he fled for his life. Alone and in crisis as a result of his bad choices, Jacob still knew very little about God. In fact, the only time that Jacob is recorded speaking God's name up to this point was when he was deceiving his father to steal Esau's family birthright.

Jacob ran from home, but he could not run from God. God visited Jacob in a dream and made promises to him, the most important of which was one of relationship: "I am with you." After meeting God, Jacob said to himself that if God would feed him, clothe him, and bring him back to the Promised Land safely, then this Speaker in his dreams would be his God. It was then that Jacob took the first steps to allow God to lead him. Rather than being just another family deity to call upon in times of crisis, Yahweh became *Jacob's* God and guided his steps throughout the rest of his life.

God wants to lead us, too! Even if you have not sought Him recently or have done so only when in crisis, God remains available and is waiting to guide you through life. Elsewhere in the Old Testament, God promises to draw near to the lowly and contrite in heart (Isaiah 57:15). We just need to humble ourselves and submit to His gracious, patient direction.

Thank You, God, for offering to lead me. In every situation, help me learn to yield to Your loving guidance.

– Reflect –

Read Genesis 28:10–22.

1. Why does God allow His followers to fall into crisis situations?

2. How can a familial legacy of faith potentially be hurtful to our relationship with God? How can one be helpful?

About the Author

CC Day was born in Alabama and grew up watching the faithfulness of his great-grandmother, whose walk with God still inspires generations of his family, with each family member developing his or her own relationship with God. CC is married to his incomparable love and partner of his life and faith walk, Cheryl.

God Cares

– DAY 6 –

Be Confident in God's Care

"So do not fear, for I am with you; do not be dismayed, for I am your God. I will strengthen you and help you; I will uphold you with my righteous right hand." (Isaiah 41:10)

Life gets so busy and overwhelming at times. With those busy seasons comes fear of the unknown, increased stress, and the sense that you are disappointing everyone around you.

Isaiah shows us how to overcome those fears and realize that God cares about us. Even when we feel like we are letting others down or like they are letting us down, fear does not have to overtake us.

You may not be in that season right now. Maybe you are afraid because you are waiting on something, and that waiting is making you nervous or anxious. In your waiting, remember that God cares. He is there to lift you up when you fall and to comfort you in every season of life.

When fears and anxieties come to steal your confidence, remember the promise of God from Isaiah 41:10: "For I am with you." Even when the weight of the world comes crashing down on your shoulders, when your struggles seem like much more than you can bear, God's Word tells you not to fear. Do not let your anxieties overwhelm you; instead, hope in God as He works through those seasons of struggle. Learn from your fear and learn to trust that God will take care of you and wrap you in His arms—even when all you want to do is curl up in a ball because it seems like the only comfort from the storm of fear.

God's message to Israel in today's passage is a message to each of us. When you feel alone, realize that God has called you to Himself. When you feel unwanted, remember that God says you are chosen by Him. Though others may reject you, God declares that He has not rejected you. In Israel's case, the people had been unfaithful, yet God's actions sprang from His own faithfulness. He is faithful still.

Verse 10 records another promise God gives us: "I will strengthen you and help you." When you feel weak, afraid, ashamed, or distraught, run to God. Let Him be your strength. Let Him carry you when you feel you cannot go on. Let Him be the guiding light in your darkest times.

Seek His care, and receive the strength and help He brings.

Father, help me to trust You with my fears and to know I am not alone in the storms of this life.

– Reflect –

Read Isaiah 41:8–10.

1. When you feel afraid, to what or whom do you instinctively turn?
2. How can you trust God instead of letting fear run your life?

About the Author

Mercedes Rich is a radio host, producer, and amateur chef (in her free time). Most importantly, Mercedes is a child of God and is constantly learning what it means to chase after and live for Him in every moment. Mercedes's favorite Scripture verses are Proverbs 19:21 and Romans 12:2.

– DAY 7 –
Give God Your Worries

"Cast all your anxiety on him because he cares for you." (1 Peter 5:7)

Anxiety has always been one of my biggest struggles; I am anxious even as I write this devotional! When I get anxious, my body tenses up. I rely on that tension to feel like I am in control over the situation and like I can solve the problem I am facing. However, trying to maintain control over my surroundings and situation does more to harm than it does to help. If I get too tense, I start shaking, which is obviously bad for me, and, typically, when I try to take control, things go in exactly the opposite way than I want them to. That is because trying to be in control is exactly the opposite of what Scripture commands us to do. Instead, we are supposed to rely on God and remember that *He* is in control.

Today's verse, 1 Peter 5:7, encapsulates this scriptural command well. Peter tells us to cast all our anxiety on God. Anxiety, whether we recognize it or not, is something we all struggle with, and God tells us to cast it on Him. He alone knows what is best for us, and He works everything out for our good. This does not mean everything will always go the way we hope. Jesus promised we will have troubles in this life. But we can have faith that even our troubles are part of God's bigger plan and purpose for us.

In verses 5–6, Peter urges us to have humility. He writes that we should clothe ourselves with humility toward each other and humble ourselves before God because God shows favor to the humble. Giving God our worries is an example of this. By telling God, "I trust You with this situation," we are each giving Him our circumstances and admitting that we cannot control them. This also helps us realize that we need not worry about what we cannot control or about what others think of us.

We are told to wear humility like clothing and to do so toward one another. In other words, humility is a choice, and others benefit when we display it. Showing humility to others encourages them to respond in humility as well. As we encourage one another toward humility, we will get better at giving our anxieties to God and at walking in faith and fellowship before Him.

Anxiety can lead to pride because anxious worry keeps our focus on ourselves. But when we turn to God and give Him our worries, we are freed from pride through humble trust and submission to His loving care.

God cares for you, so why not give Him your worries today?

God, help me to humble myself and give You my worries, believing that You truly do care for me.

– Reflect –

Read 1 Peter 5:5–7.

1. How does clinging to your anxieties lead to pride?
2. What worries do you need to give to God?

About the Author

Abigail Esch is fourteen years old and lives in Germantown, Maryland. She has attended Redland Baptist Church with her family for nine years. She is homeschooled, and she loves Jesus, flamingos, music, Chick-fil-A, and outreach. She also practices Tang Soo Do martial arts, plays piano and handbells, and sings in the church youth choir.

– DAY 8 –

Model God's Care to Others

"In humility value others above yourselves, not looking to your own interests but each of you to the interests of the others." (Philippians 2:3–4)

Few delights in this world compare with seeing the look of pure joy, love, and appreciation on someone's face. A person's expression of delight radiates to others, and they all share the cheerful moment. A child who receives an unexpected gift will often respond with unabashed delight. Similarly, those who receive a kind, heartfelt gesture in times of trouble may display a look of deep appreciation. These reactions reflect on the giver of the gift, and, more importantly, on the love of God.

During His earthly ministry, Jesus performed daily acts of love and kindness. His actions met the physical, spiritual, and emotional needs of the people He encountered. He healed the sick. He comforted the grieving or troubled. He forgave sins. These were not random acts of kindness. Rather, Jesus perceived the heart and soul of each person and then acted purposefully to meet his or her individual needs. What a wonderful experience it must have been to encounter Jesus and be renewed with a cleansed heart, an invigorated body, and an uplifted spirit! It is no wonder people came running to Jesus with their needs, believing in faith that He was the Son of God, and then went away praising our God in heaven.

How can we emulate Jesus's ministry in our own lives? How can we look to the "interests of others" and meet their individual needs? Everyone in this world can benefit from a listening ear, a kind word of encouragement, and a prayer of support. We can take others a meal when they are overwhelmed, visit those who are sick in the hospital, share a cup of coffee with one who is burdened, and serve those who cannot care for themselves. Sometimes, you may not need to do anything more than sit by someone's side as a friend with a listening ear. As you have received comfort from God in times of trouble, you can also give comfort and minister to those around you in His name (2 Corinthians 1:3–4).

As you look to serve the needs and interests of others, you will be expressing the love of God to them. Even your smallest act of service toward others may touch their souls in ways you cannot even begin to imagine. Demonstrate your personal love and care for others by meeting their needs, and do it all in the name of Christ.

Lord, reveal to me a person whom I may help today in some way, and enable me to demonstrate Your love, care, and peace.

– Reflect –

Read Philippians 2:1–8.

1. What are some of the gifts and comforts you have received that you can use in acts of service toward others?

2. How can you show God's love to others in a practical manner?

About the Author

David and Peggy Roney have been members of Redland Baptist Church for nearly thirty years. Three generations of their family belong to Redland. They are both involved in the church's worship services through its various instrumental and choir groups. They also regularly attend or lead Bible studies in which Christian growth is emphasized.

– DAY 9 –

Bring Every Issue to God

"Pray continually, give thanks in all circumstances; for this is God's will for you in Christ Jesus." (1 Thessalonians 5:17–18)

I remember one day when I could not find my journal. I looked everywhere for it! Finally, without any other place to search, I prayed in desperation and asked God to help me find it. Amazingly, within a moment, I realized where my journal was. I knew God had helped me find it, but I did not take time to thank Him for directing my thoughts to its location. I simply began to write in it as though nothing had happened. That night, as I lay in bed, I remembered my mistake. The situation was a reminder to me of our need not only to give thanks but also to pray without ceasing.

"Praying without ceasing" is something we often forget to do. We go through the day without praying until something bad happens: We lose important papers, we cannot find our keys, or we forget the answer to a test question. When this happens, we send up a quick prayer, and, graciously, God often helps us. But then sometimes we go on as if nothing happened.

Many of us go through this cycle of forgetting to pray until a challenge or hardship arises that we cannot handle on our own. It is as if we treat prayer like calling 911—we forget all about it until the moment we need help.

Today's passage explains that God's will for us is that we *continually* pray to Him. This does not mean that every moment of the day we should have our heads bowed and eyes closed while speaking directly to God. However, it does mean that we should pray regularly and at every opportunity, always seeking to maintain an *attitude* of prayer.

Whenever an issue arises, we should immediately pray about it; this is good and right to do! But we should also be quick to give thanks to God for His answers to our prayers—whether they bring joy or pain.

Because God loves to hear from His children, He asks us to spend regular time talking with Him. We can talk to Him anytime. In other words, God asks us to bring every issue to Him and to recognize thankfully that He is ready to help us in every situation we face.

Jesus, help me to keep my heart focused on You so that I never stop praying.

– Reflect –

Read 1 Thessalonians 5:17–18.

1. When you experience difficulties, to whom or what do you tend to turn first?
2. How does giving thanks in all circumstances help you trust God's will?

About the Author

Olivia Freeman is ten years old and has grown up at Redland Baptist Church. She loves to play and has a spunky personality. At home, she enjoys reading, journaling, making crafts, and playing with her dog, Bingo. At church, Olivia often has a smile on her face and likes to talk with people.

– DAY 10 –

Receive God's Care Through Others

"I can do all this through him who gives me strength." (Philippians 4:13)

The year 2000 was difficult for me, to put it lightly. So many simultaneous life changes caused by the natural consequences of my sin put my emotions into a tailspin. Every day, my thoughts were a jumbled cloud of guilt, shame, sadness, and worry. Although I had sought forgiveness from God and knew He heard my prayers, I still had to bear the consequences of my sin publicly. My church family could have removed me from their fellowship and turned their backs on me for what I had done, but by God's grace, they did not.

Instead, they embraced Redland's mission of being "grace-driven people for a grace-needing world." Those in the body of Christ at Redland surrounded me with grace as they showed me God's love and care. My circumstances were less than ideal, and that season was not easy, fun, or comfortable. But through the kindness of other believers, I was able to see God's provision in my current and past circumstances—both the good and the not-so-good. The church came together to pray for me and my family and to bring monetary and material support. Through this care, I came to understand better how to live in a God-honoring way through my Savior, Christ Jesus, who gives me strength in every circumstance.

In today's passage, we see how Paul thanked those in the congregation at Philippi for remembering him in their prayers and for their gifts to him. Paul was not presently in great need, even though he was under house arrest in Rome. Nevertheless, he took the opportunity to offer thanks and testify to God's provision throughout his life. Paul told the people how he had "learned to be content whatever the circumstances" (v. 11).

As the body of Christ, we are called to love all people. While this love may be shown in many ways—through witnessing to unbelievers, serving those in need, visiting the sick, or caring for widows and orphans—this love must also be shown within the community of believers by coming alongside one another in our moments of need. I have received such care, and I know the support and nourishment it has brought to my faith. God empowers us to serve one another, which in turn enables us to flourish amid life's most difficult circumstances.

Lord God, thank You for being my provider in every circumstance and for giving me strength to honor You by caring for others.

– Reflect –

Read Philippians 4:10–13.

1. Think of a time when others helped and cared for you. How did God give you the strength to get through your circumstance as a result of this care?

2. Can you think of someone who may need to be shown the love of God right now?

About the Author

Christy Horton joined Redland Baptist Church in 1994 and has been actively involved in various ministries, primarily in music ministry. Christy and Matt Horton were married at Redland and raised their two boys, Wesley and Daniel, as part of the Redland church family. Their niece Alexis joined the Horton household in 2021 and is also part of the Redland church family. Christy also serves as Redland's administrative assistant and loves supporting the work of the church in this way.

God Provides

– DAY 11 –

Practice Contentment with God's Provision

"And my God will meet all your needs according to the riches of his glory in Christ Jesus."
(Philippians 4:19)

In 2000, my family and I were living in Conway, New Hampshire. While we were there, a group from Redland Baptist Church (RBC) came to help our church with summer programs, and the people of RBC left a great impression on me. A few years later, after we had moved our family to Colorado, I took a consulting contract in McLean, Virginia, which is about thirty-five minutes from RBC. The first week I was in McLean, I reached out to Bill, one of the members from the RBC mission trip group, to tell him that I was in the area. He immediately responded, "I will pick you up on Sunday for church." That began the second phase of my relationship with RBC.

As a consultant traveling in from another state, I was very conscious of expenses. The contract was not paying as much as I had hoped, and I found myself without a means of personal transportation during my stay. I had to ride into work with a fellow contractor who was staying with family nearby. Bill was excited to connect me with two other RBC members, who graciously gave me a ride to church every Sunday and Wednesday. In a season when I was in need, God provided community and connection through the kindness of fellow believers.

Just as the Philippians were a blessing to Paul in his ministry, RBC was a blessing to me during the early days of my time attending the church in Maryland. Over the years, God has provided for me financially and spiritually in many ways so that I now have the opportunity to be His blessing to others as well. As I have learned to be content and trust God, I have seen His hand on my life, and I know that He wants me to be like the Philippians, seeking out ways I can be a blessing to others.

In today's passage, Paul is willing to receive the help that the Philippian believers are willing to give. God's children often find it easier either to give help or to receive help, but few are good at both. Which is more difficult for you? If we have trouble receiving help, it may be a symptom of pride. Alternatively, unwillingness to help and love others may reveal selfishness in our hearts. One of the unexpected blessings of being part of a church family is that God uses our church relationships to teach us how to show and receive love from other believers.

As part of God's family, we can experience fellowship with other believers by sharing in the joy of giving and receiving help and of caring for one another in different seasons of life. Whatever season you are in, let God prepare your heart to give or to receive what is needed.

Father, help me to be content with Your provision and to see how You can use me to bless others.

– Reflect –

Read Philippians 4:14–20.

1. When have you needed something that you could not provide for yourself? Did you find it hard to be content and trust God to provide what you needed? Were you willing to ask for or receive help from others?

2. How can God use you to be a blessing to others who are waiting for His provision?

About the Author

Rob Burba is a native Texan who moved to Maryland for work in 2003. He and his wife, Cheryl, have enjoyed serving in many different roles at Redland. Rob is most involved in teaching, leading within the men's ministry, being involved in the music ministry, serving as a deacon, and ministering as the adult ministry director.

– DAY 12 –

Thank God for His Provision

"Wealth and honor come from you; you are the ruler of all things. In your hands are strength and power to exalt and give strength to all."
(1 Chronicles 29:12)

Our family story is rooted in knowing God as the Ruler of all things. In 2006, just as my husband, Pedro, and I had learned that we were finally going to have a baby, Pedro lost his job. As a preschool teacher, I barely took home enough money to cover our basic needs. Pedro was able to find another job that paid on commission, but his boss was frequently unable to pay us. As our bills piled up, we doubled down on prayer.

One Sunday morning, Pedro and I had to decide how to use the tiny amount of gas left in our car. We could go to church, or we could wait until the next day and drive to Pedro's work to ask for his commissions. We chose to go to church to pray. As we were leaving the parking lot to head back home, a church deacon stopped us and said that he had been led by God to give us twenty dollars. It was exactly what we needed to be able to put gas in our car for work the next day.

On Monday, Pedro dropped me off at the preschool and went to work. As he walked in, his boss said, "I am so glad you are here! I was about to call you so you could pick up your check." The check included all the back pay that Pedro was owed! All our needs and wants were covered by God's grace.

Later, on Easter Sunday, I was rushed to the hospital with pregnancy complications. Our child was to be born prematurely, and the doctors gave us no hope that he would survive. But by now, we knew to trust God that His will would be done. We had already faced many difficult moments in our lives, and each time God had provided in a way we had not expected. Our son, Josue, was born that day. He struggled to breathe and had cerebral thrombosis, or blood clots in the brain. Even through this hardship, we still worshiped God.

Josue is now a completely healthy seventeen-year-old, and we still worship God, giving thanks for His provisions. We praise God, knowing that all blessings come from Him.

As King David praised the Lord, he modeled giving back to God what God had given him. His example leads us to join in worship and in giving, as all that we have comes from God.

Heavenly Father, with a grateful heart I praise Your glorious name for Your faithful provision.

– Reflect –

Read 1 Chronicles 29:10–13.

1. Worship is a response to God's work. How is acknowledging that everything we have comes from God a form of worship?

2. How can our struggles become opportunities to build a relationship with God?

About the Author

Raquel Torres Fernandez and her family moved from Puerto Rico to Maryland in 2008. Raquel, Pedro, and their two sons love Redland Baptist Church and have been actively worshiping and serving since 2012 within the children's and young adult ministries. God continues to meet their needs bountifully.

– DAY 13 –

Walk in God's Strength

"For the Lord God is a sun and shield; the Lord bestows favor and honor; no good thing does he withhold from those whose walk is blameless."
(Psalm 84:11)

What do you do when the bottom drops out?

We can be easily overwhelmed by the daily chaos of the world happening around us. Because most of us wrestle with tight schedules and full daily routines, we tend to push away the distressing topics and discord of life, preferring to keep difficult things at a comfortable distance. But sometimes what we wish to avoid arrives front and center, refusing to be ignored.

Just when we think we have it all together, our comfortable, controlled lives collapse around us. Your house is flooded, your car is wrecked, your identity is stolen, your job is gone, and all your retirement funds and investments have been taken. Then, to make matters worse, someone you love receives the dreaded cancer diagnosis.

Believe it or not, all these crises have happened to me. Countless difficulties and relational struggles have come my way, things that are common to all men. At my lowest point, it seemed like all the good things of life were being withheld from me, which caused me to analyze my relationship with God. I had to reconsider who I thought God was, how He worked, and whether I was committed to Him. Did I prefer to live for myself and for my agenda with my understanding—or did I wish to grasp the height and width and depth of who God is and what His agenda is for my life?

It seems very hard and scary sometimes, but the safest place to be on the planet is in the center of God's perfect will, walking confidently with Him hemming you in, before and behind. In my experience, He loves to flex His muscles and show off for His expectant children. When we can figure things out and work them out on our own, we simply do not look for God. The challenge for each of us is to go past the point of comfort, reach for something beyond ourselves, and be bold. See the impossible situation thrown at you for what it is: your next chance to be captivated and amazed by our awesome God!

Lord, thank You for knowing what is truly good for me and for providing everything I need. Help me to see You through my difficult circumstances and to understand that Your provisions are good, even when I am disappointed with my situation.

– Reflect –

Read Psalm 84.

1. Looking back on your life, where do you recognize God's perfect answer and provision that you may have misunderstood at the time?
2. Are your ways completely committed to the Lord, and is your walk blameless before Him?

About the Author

Michael Avers is an adrenaline junkie with a body too old to do extreme sports. Therefore, he spends his days searching the Scriptures to see how to recognize, inspire, and participate in God-ordained activities and relationships that have eternal significance. Michael is married to Silvia, and together they have four kids.

– DAY 14 –

View God as Your Loving Father

"See what great love the Father has lavished on us, that we should be called children of God! And that is what we are! The reason the world does not know us is that it did not know him."
(1 John 3:1)

I have a treasure trove of memories of my dad. I adored him. When I was a child, I loved to slip my feet into his dress shoes and clomp around the house. I loved the way he "held" my hand, not enveloping it but allowing me to wrap my entire hand around just two of his fingers. My dad made me feel safe, protected, and small in the very best of ways. But one of my sweetest memories of my dad happened when I was no longer a child.

My heart was broken—shattered in a way that happens only when a "first love" comes to an end. I sat on the floor of my childhood bedroom next to a wooden crate, filled with photographs of the previous five years. I pulled the photos out one by one, ripping them in half, hoping that each jagged tear would somehow inversely bind up one of the tears in my heart. My dad, not one to show emotions easily, came into my room. There was no condescending look, no patronizing words about all the other fish in the sea. In fact, there were no words at all that I remember. There was just my dad, folding his long legs underneath him to sit beside me in my pain, pulling me into his arms and reminding me that I was not alone. I was held. I was understood. I was profoundly loved.

A million moments like this one made it so easy for me to learn to see God as my loving Father.

I know quite well that many others are not as fortunate. To those people, I would suggest letting your mind run free to imagine the father you *wish* you had. A father who adores you? God is that one. One who understands every situation? The very God who took on flesh understands life's pressures. A father whose discipline is only and always for your benefit? God's loving discipline transforms us from one degree of glory to another. A father who would never abandon you? God promises never, ever to leave or forsake you.

Because of the adoption secured for us through Jesus's death and Resurrection, we can be called the precious children of God. We are held close, we are completely understood, we are lovingly transformed, and we are perfectly and deeply loved. This good news can help you relax in the arms of your loving Father.

Father God, thank You for being just that: Father God. Help me to feel Your love and guidance today.

– Reflect –

Read 1 John 3:1–3.

1. What fatherly quality do you most need to see in God?

2. If you truly saw God as your Father, in what way would that change your life?

About the Author

Cyndi Word is a mother to three amazing young adults who have grown up at Redland Baptist Church. She has been a Redland member for much longer than she cares to admit, as it shows her age! Three generations of her family are involved at Redland.

– DAY 15 –

Trust God with Tomorrow

"His compassions never fail. They are new every morning; great is your faithfulness."
(Lamentations 3:22–23)

Have you ever become consumed with worry about the future? This worry most often comes when we feel unsure about what the future holds. Hours after having our first child, my husband and I learned that our son had Down syndrome. This was a shock to both of us because it had not been diagnosed during my pregnancy. I was only twenty-six at the time and was not considered at high risk of having a child with this condition. My first thoughts were about what the future would look like for my son and for our family. I was worried that I would not get to enjoy the milestones that other parents celebrate with their children or that my son would not have any friends. My fears were based on the unknown.

As I prayed about my child, God gave me peace and reminded me that I did not need to know everything that would happen in the future. He told me that He would provide His grace each day as needed. I began to meditate on the verses from today's passage in Lamentations, and I reminded myself that my faithful God is bigger than any challenges I face.

At the time of this writing, my son has just finished high school. While he has significant disabilities, he lives a full life with lots of activities and many friends. The fears that I had when he was born were unfounded, and God has blessed our family through our son.

Throughout the Bible, God reminds us to trust Him and not to fear. Our trust is based in the character of God. If we know that God is faithful, then we know that He will provide the daily grace we need to face each day's problems. Just as the Israelites in the wilderness went out and collected manna each morning, we are invited to seek God each day and to lay down our burdens and accept His grace. Jesus reminds us in the Sermon on the Mount that each day has enough trouble of its own, so our efforts are better spent on seeking God's Kingdom and righteousness than on worrying about tomorrow (Matthew 6:33–34).

If you are burdened by worries about your future, give them to God every morning and ask for His grace and mercy to give you the strength you need for the day ahead.

God, please take my worries and concerns from me and give me Your grace and strength for today.

– Reflect –

Read Lamentations 3:22–24.

1. Why do you think God offers His compassion to us new every morning?
2. What thoughts do you need to give to God today so that you are not burdened by worry?

About the Author

Becky McGaffin grew up at Redland Baptist Church, where she now attends with her husband and two sons. She and her husband are both high school science teachers at Damascus High School. She teaches youth Sunday school and is a deacon at the church.

God Helps

– DAY 16 –

Seek God's Wisdom for Daily Help

"For the Lord *gives wisdom; from his mouth come knowledge and understanding."*
(Proverbs 2:6)

Remember when people used to use checks to pay for things? In 1 Kings 3, shortly after Solomon became king, God appeared to him in a dream and essentially gave him what could be considered a blank check: "Ask for whatever you want me to give you" (1 Kings 3:5). Solomon asked for wisdom, and we see that wisdom on display in the book of Proverbs.

Everyone wants to be good at what they do. We feel a sense of worth when others view us as "experts" at something. How do we get to that point? The foundation of expertise in our work is knowledge. All skilled workers—doctors, scientists, engineers, craftsmen, technicians—devote time and effort to learning the information, techniques, and practices necessary for their work. When assessing others' skills, we rightly look for academic degrees, certifications, and other credentials because they lend credibility to the products and services we receive from these professionals. But earned credentials merely provide the starting point for a successful career. Expertise comes only by applying knowledge to real-world circumstances over time and by learning how to adapt to challenges.

Expertise is important for a successful career, but the complications of daily life call for wisdom. Wisdom helps us respond to situations in which the best response is often not obvious. Proverbs 2 says that wisdom comes by accepting God's words and treasuring His commands. Through the Scriptures, we learn the heart of God and see His plans and expectations for people. We also see many examples of the good and not-so-good ways people chose to act, and we discover how their choices affected them and others. Within this context of God's Word, God promises to give us wisdom.

How do we know if we are receiving God's wisdom? We will never be able to assess the wisdom of our actions by reviewing the results of alternative paths we chose not to take. But when our life choices are in line with Scripture, we can have an inner confidence that we are doing the right thing. Generally, when we walk in the light of God's wisdom, life seems to work better for us and for those around us. Proverbs 2:11–12 states, "Discretion will protect you, and understanding will guard you. Wisdom will save you from the ways of wicked men." However, even when life becomes challenging, we can still trust that walking in accordance with God's revealed Word keeps us walking in "the ways of the good" and on the "paths of the righteous" (Proverbs 2:20).

God, give me the commitment and discipline to bring Your words and commandments into my heart. As I grow to know You more fully, give me Your wisdom in every area of my life.

– Reflect –

Read Proverbs 2:1–13.

1. Do you seek God's wisdom in every part of your life? What can you do to make yourself more open to receiving God's wisdom?

2. Are there any situations in your life in which you can apply and reflect God's wisdom?

About the Author

Mike Moore has been at Redland for over twenty years, spending many of those years as a middle school Sunday school teacher. Highest among his countless blessings are an amazing wife and two amazing adult daughters.

– DAY 17 –

Call to God for His Help

"The righteous cry out, and the Lord hears them; he delivers them from all their troubles."
(Psalm 34:17)

I remember when my husband and I desperately wanted to start a family. After what seemed like an eternity, we found out we were pregnant. We were over-the-moon excited! Then, twelve weeks later, we learned that our baby's heartbeat could no longer be heard. Anger and grief coursed through us following the miscarriage. No counsel could ease the pain—not even counsel from those who had suffered the same kind of tragedy. I tried to understand why this might have happened. I read books, searched online, met with doctors, and took more vitamins. I tried every means to ensure it would not happen again, because I felt like damaged goods.

Then, during one of my afternoon runs—a familiar outlet of personal escape—I finally cried out to God in my anger and despair, asking for a child. I do not know why I waited so long to turn to God. Instead of seeking His face, I had been putting my trust in human means and in my own understanding. The Lord answered my request. Today we have three healthy, beautiful boys.

David wrote Psalm 34 when he fled from King Saul into Philistine territory. After David was recognized by the enemy, he escaped by feigning insanity. Just as I did, David also poured his heart out to God while on the run, entrusting God with the outcome. He had already experienced tragedy. He had lost his military position, his known associates had been put to death, and King Saul continued to pursue David, seeking to end his life. Despite these threats, David chose to fear God rather than man.

David later showed his reverence for God by sparing Saul's life when he had an easy opportunity to kill him. He chose not to kill Saul, because he knew that the right action involved continuing to serve the man whom God had anointed king. David trusted God to make things right; he knew he did not have to take the situation into his own hands.

Being righteous involves living in a right relationship with God, who wants a deep connection with His children. He desires that we rely on Him, follow Him, and submit to and obey Him. He will always answer when we cry out to Him. We may not always receive the answer we hope for, but we can trust in God's close presence during our brokenness.

God, thank You for always hearing my prayers. Help me not to lean on my own understanding but to call upon You always.

– Reflect –

Read Psalm 34:4–18.

1. When have you tried to face a difficult situation without relying on God?

2. What reminders will help you rely more on God? How can your trust in God help others, especially during hard times?

About the Author

Sara Carbonell met her husband, Gabriel (Gabe), shortly after college and began attending Redland with Gabe's family. They later married and made Redland their church home. After the birth of her second child, Sara rededicated her life to God and joined Redland through baptism. She and her family enjoy serving in Redland's children's and youth ministries.

– DAY 18 –

Face Your Battles with God's Help

"You will not have to fight this battle. Take up your positions; stand firm and see the deliverance the LORD will give you, Judah and Jerusalem. Do not be afraid; do not be discouraged. Go out to face them tomorrow, and the LORD will be with you." (2 Chronicles 20:17)

We are the Stricklands, and we follow Christ. We have followed Christ in the good times, we have followed Christ in the bad times, and we will continue to follow Christ in whatever will come our way. We both grew up in rural towns. We both went to college and reveled in the carnal pleasures of this world, living in that state for decades. Then, Christ found us in our early thirties. As you may already know, finding Christ is not the end of the story but the beginning. Jesus does not simply show up and make everything better. It is a little more complicated than that.

During our time as Christians, we have experienced tremendous blessings and crippling trials. It is easy to believe the promises of God when things are good, but when things are bad, it is not so easy. On May 16, 2020, our fifth child was born with a rare genetic malformation, and the doctors told us that her disability was "incompatible with life." They tried to counsel us on "interventions," but we instead chose faith that God would heal her, deeply desiring that it be on this side of the veil. Countless, almost ceaseless prayers, tears, and screams occurred during that very short, painful season. Vivian Hope lived only six weeks, but her life forever changed our family for the better.

The Lord tells us not to be afraid or discouraged. While we still struggle with fear, discontentment, anger, depression, and grief, 2 Chronicles 20:9 assures us that when we cry out in our distress, the Lord will hear us and save us. "We do not know what to do, but our eyes are on you" (2 Chronicles 20:12).

God can use tremendous adversity to teach us complete surrender and grow us in sanctification. He can use any number of circumstances—good and bad—to accomplish His work in us. Through each of these experiences, we are asked to stand our ground, fixing our eyes on Christ.

As Jahaziel says to the people of God in this passage,

> You will not have to fight this battle. Take up your positions; stand firm and see the deliverance the LORD will give you, Judah and Jerusalem. Do not be afraid; do not be discouraged. Go out to face them tomorrow, and the LORD will be with you. (2 Chronicles 20:17)

We face each new day because this is His story; our God is the author of all our tomorrows, and He promises to be with us. When we follow Christ, He will faithfully deliver each of us at just the right time, according to His plans. And we will no longer need to fight, for the battle has already been won.

God, thank You for fighting on my behalf in all circumstances. May I be encouraged, keep my eyes fixed on You, and stand firm, knowing the best is yet to come.

– Reflect –

Read 2 Chronicles 20:5–17.

1. What was happening when Jehoshaphat called out to God for help? How does this relate to a situation in your life?

2. Think of a time in your past when God's hand was on a difficult situation but you were unaware of it at the time. Take a moment to thank God for His faithfulness in that trial.

About the Author

Kimberly Strickland was introduced to the ladies Bible study at Redland in 2015. After attending for several years and loving the Redland people, the Stricklands became members of the church in 2021. Kimberly's husband, Jason, serves on the tech team and assists with Grace Groups. Kimberly enjoys serving and helping with the thrift store ministry, Grace in Store; recreation ministries; and American Heritage Girls, in which both their girls participate. The children enjoy choir and handbells, as well as any and all Redland summer camps.

– DAY 19 –

Set Your Hope in God

"Our help is in the name of the Lord, the Maker of heaven and earth." (Psalm 124:8)

Our devotion today is on Psalm 124, which was written by David, the shepherd king of Israel. The first three verses of this psalm paint a picture using "what if" questions:

> If the Lord had not been on our side—let Israel say—if the Lord had not been on our side when people attacked us, they would have swallowed us alive, when their anger flared against us. (Psalm 124:1–3)

These three verses by themselves remind us that if the Lord were not on our side, we would be totally without hope. But because He is on our side, we should set our hope on Him at all times.

Verses 4 and 5 paint a dramatic picture of what could befall us, were it not for the Lord's help: "The flood would have engulfed us, the torrent would have swept over us, the raging waters would have swept us away." The wording here evokes images of natural disasters, like the devastating storms and floods we have seen in recent years.

In these verses, David the warrior king was describing a real battle against God's enemies, but we can still apply the truth of these inspiring words in our own lives. Do you feel at times that everything is against you? Perhaps it is an irritable boss, a debt you just cannot find a way to pay, or a broken relationship. Maybe you or your family are facing an actual storm or similar disaster, and there seems to be no one to help you survive. We may be tempted to give up hope, but knowing we need help is the first step to finding hope again. Set your hope in God so that faith in the Lord will remind you help is on its way!

Verses 6 and 7 show the result of trusting in the Lord: "Praise be to the LORD, who has not let us be torn by their teeth. We have escaped like a bird from the fowler's snare; the snare has been broken, and we have escaped." And the reason this can happen is summed up perfectly in our focal point verse: "Our help is in the name of the LORD, the Maker of heaven and earth" (Psalm 124:8).

What a comfort that we can know that all our help emanates from our Creator God, who made the heavens and the earth! If God could do all that, He is more than able to grant us the hope and help we need.

You have probably heard these famous opening lyrics from a pop song of my youth (so many years ago!): "Help! I need somebody. Help! Not just anybody. Help! You know, I need someone—help!"

John Lennon, the singer-songwriter, was looking to other people for help because he did not quite understand that the help he *truly* needed was from the Lord, who created the heavens and earth. Hope and help are found in Him alone.

Lord, give me courage and confidence to know that all my hope and help come from You!

– Reflect –

Read Psalm 124.

1. Why do we often wait to ask God for help only when going through difficulties?
2. What happens when we seek His help daily to face whatever comes, knowing He is on our side?

About the Author

Don Dunnevant has had the distinct joy and privilege to serve as minister of music for churches in Texas, Maryland, and his home state of Virginia for thirty years. Don was a letter carrier in Rockville for twenty-two years, retiring nearly nine years ago. Don is blessed with a wonderful wife of thirty-six years. Don and his wife have been members of Redland since 2011, where they enjoy the fellowship, worship, and Bible study so very much. Don sings in the sanctuary choir as well as the National Christian Choir, writing and arranging songs for the Lord's glory.

– DAY 20 –

Rely on God's Indwelling Help

"And I will ask the Father, and he will give you another advocate to help you and be with you forever." (John 14:16)

"This is way outside of my comfort zone!"

When was the last time you said those words? Three years ago, God called me beyond my comfort zone in a very unexpected way. In 2020, the COVID-19 pandemic shut down many church ministries, including the Kids for Praise children's choirs and the other music groups at Redland. For two years, this historically thriving ministry lay dormant. During this period, the directors retired, which meant that new leadership would be required in order for the ministry to return. A big question also loomed in my mind: Would there still be an interest in children's choirs following the shutdown? I was hoping for a revival of sorts, but could it happen?

The challenge of finding new leaders for the elementary-aged group persisted at the church; no one stepped forward to lead. After much prayer, the Lord impressed on me that He wanted me to lead this group. This was what stretched me out of my comfort zone. While I have led numerous musical groups during my many years of ministry, I had never been the lead director of a children's choir. I wondered how my male, baritone voice could demonstrate the vocal needs of the children's higher-pitched treble voices. Could I make the experience engaging enough to keep the children interested? Would we even have enough children return to have a choir?

While personal doubts continuously swirled in my mind, I was reminded of a sermon I had heard years ago in which the preacher said, "God will never call you to a task or lead you into an experience that you can do on your own." This wise preacher reminded us—reminded *me*—that God always leads us into more dependence on Him, no matter the circumstance. And in that dependency, God will provide all that is needed—Himself—to lead, guide, and support us. John 14:16 underscored this truth in my mind. I was comforted to know that I could rely on the indwelling presence of the Holy Spirit through each step, in both preparing for and leading this group of precious children.

The promise of the Holy Spirit, our Advocate, is available to all of Christ's followers. We can rely on Him to be present at all times, even in moments of need, distress, loss, loneliness, or uncertainty.

Precious Lord, thank You for the forever promise of being with me, especially when I am faced with challenging circumstances.

– Reflect –

Read John 14:15–17.

1. When was the last time you were outside your comfort zone? How would you describe your sense of God's presence with you during that time?

2. When experiencing life's challenges, we are not alone. God is present, and He wants us to depend on Him. What are some ways you can rely on Him in whatever you are going through right now?

About the Author

Bill Archer is a Virginia native and has been the minister of worship at Redland since 2009. His Maryland connection was attending the University of Maryland, where he met his wife, Ava. Bill and Ava have three grown children and three grandchildren. Ava has recently retired from Montgomery County Public Schools.

God Saves

– DAY 21 –

Look to God Alone for Deliverance

"When you pass through the waters, I will be with you; and when you pass through the rivers, they will not sweep over you. When you walk through the fire, you will not be burned; the flames will not set you ablaze." (Isaiah 43:2)

What has God saved me from? He has certainly been gracious to save me from the punishment for my sins that would have separated me from Him for eternity. I thank Him so much for rescuing me through the death and Resurrection of His Son, Jesus, and for helping me put my faith in Him!

God has also saved me from earthly danger. I would have died during a house fire in the middle of the night if God had not awoken my family and me in time to get us out safely. The fire destroyed most of our home, but my family and I were unscathed. Ever since that night, I have praised Him for His protection. He has shown me that He still has a purpose for my life, as He could have easily called me home to heaven, but He spared my life instead.

Isaiah 43:2 uses imagery to describe situations that could easily overwhelm us and knock us down.

These images may refer to big crises that come up in life, like house fires, but I think they can also represent times when we feel upset, angry, or overwhelmed in any situation throughout the day. Maybe someone tailgates us or cuts us off in traffic, or perhaps an unkind word is said to us when we did nothing wrong. Whenever we are sinned against, we start to feel indignant and upset. We want to retaliate, to seek justice for the wrong that has been done to us. And sometimes, our form of "justice" is thinking angry thoughts about the offender.

In these moments, the Lord can help us recognize when we start to feel angry and remind us that He is with us. The Holy Spirit may bring verses to mind about forgiving our brothers or loving our enemies so that we respond to mistreatment with compassion and prayer. The Lord does not just save us from disasters or moments of crisis; He also delivers us from temptation as we face mundane, daily irritations, too. In every moment, we can call on Him, asking Him to help us forgive others or show them grace, and we can look to Him to restore our joy each time it is needed throughout the day.

Dear Lord, when I am tempted to stay upset with someone or something, please restore my joy and peace in You and help me to forgive that person.

– Reflect –

Read Isaiah 43:1–7.

1. What, or who, causes you to become angry, annoyed, or upset during a typical day?
2. How might God want to change your perspective on the people who often upset you? How can you pray blessings on them instead of staying upset?

About the Author

Rachel Freese grew up as a missionary kid in West Africa. Her family was blessed by the Redland congregation's generosity and hospitality through the church's mission Furlough House in Africa and their warmth during her family's stateside visits, which led Rachel to join the church in 2020. As a member of Redland, she enjoys taking part in the music, young adult, and children's ministries.

– DAY 22 –

Believe That God Forgives Sins

"For God so loved the world that he gave his one and only Son, that whoever believes in him shall not perish but have eternal life." (John 3:16)

Today's passage comes from Christ's dialogue with Nicodemus, a respected member of the Sanhedrin, which served as a sort of religious Supreme Court in first-century Israel. This same group would later arrest Jesus, put Him through a show trial, convict Him of blasphemy, and turn Him over to the Roman authorities to be crucified.

Of the 31,102 verses in the Bible, John 3:16 may be the most popular, or at least the most familiar. It is seen often on banners at sporting events, on T-shirts, on bumper stickers, and in other prominent places. But even if you have heard this famous verse a thousand times before, take a moment to consider each phrase carefully:

- *"For God so loved the world"*: This is a powerful, succinct statement of the entire gospel. This verse speaks to God's unmerited love for each one of us, regardless of what we have done.
- *"That he gave his one and only Son"*: The breadth of God's love is manifest in this phrase. Just

as God supplied a sacrificial lamb in place of Abraham's son, Isaac, so He supplied His own Son—the Lamb of God—for all of humanity.

- *"That whoever believes in him"*: The gift of God's love is available to everyone, but it comes only through belief in Jesus. To believe means much more than having intellectual awareness or agreement. It means to trust in, to rely on, and to cling to Jesus as your only hope of having peace with God.
- *"Shall not perish"*: This phrase describes the intention of God's love, which saves man from eternal destruction. Not wanting fallen humanity to perish, God extends the gift of salvation in Jesus Christ.
- *"But have eternal life."*: The duration of God's love reaches to the furthest distance of eternity. The love we receive among people may fade or turn, but God's love will never change.

What a stunning portrait of the entire narrative of redemption! God graciously invites us to come as we are, promising that, when we do, He will not turn us away.

Lord, as I ponder on Your unfathomable love, I am humbled by the sacrifice of Your Son, Jesus Christ. He came not to condemn but to save and to offer redemption to all—including me, a broken soul in need of Your healing touch. Thank You for the salvation You offer! Now, help me do Your will.

– Reflect –

Read John 3:16–18.

1. If John 3:16 is familiar to you, how does slowing down and considering each phrase of the verse help to shift your perspective and provide new insights?

2. What does John 3:16–18 reveal about God's heart for us? What does it reveal about the heart of fallen humanity toward God?

About the Author

Bob Michael is a lifelong resident of Montgomery County and has been a member at Redland Baptist Church for over forty years. Over the years, he has enjoyed teaching adult Sunday school—now Grace Groups—at the church. He is married to Ann, and they have three grown children. They love spending time with their nine grandkids.

– DAY 23 –

Place Faith in God's Mercy Alone

"He saved us . . . so that, having been justified by his grace, we might become heirs having the hope of eternal life." (Titus 3:5–7)

Eşref Armağan is an amazing person. Born blind, Armağan nevertheless has become an accomplished artist. He took to drawing as a young boy, helped by his father to assess shapes and recreate them on a page. Later, he began to paint with his fingers and experimented with color tones. Now, he can even correctly guess the type and color of flowers by their scent! A quick search for some of Armağan's works would be well worth your time.

Armağan's paintings are far more beautiful than any I could produce. Though blind, he "sees" the world in a way that I cannot. An MRI scan even showed that, while Armağan paints, the visual cortex of his brain activates just like that of a person with sight.[1] Armağan paints a world he cannot see but that he knows exists. His paintings express hope in the beauty of the "invisible" world.

God offers us the hope of another world—an eternal home with Him in heaven. We cannot yet see it, but we know it exists. Our access to this invisible world comes not from our own accomplishments but only from God's mercy. The apostle Paul wrote in his letter to Titus and the believers in Crete that God had saved them and made them heirs to the promise of eternal life through Jesus their Savior. By placing faith in Jesus as Savior, anyone can have the hope of eternal life. Through faith, anyone can have sight.

If you have already placed your faith in Jesus, you have been given the ability to "see" the hope of heaven! Earlier in Titus 3, Paul explains that when we trust in Jesus, we are washed, born again, and renewed by the Holy Spirit. We receive through Jesus a taste of the life that is to come—a glimpse of our future home, the eternal world that awaits. Every Christian now has an assignment, like Armağan, to paint a world we know exists but cannot fully see. By living out our faith in Jesus, we "paint" a picture of the world to come for others to see so that they will also place their faith in Jesus and receive new life in Him.

If you have not yet placed your faith in Jesus, it is easy to do. Simply repent, or turn away, from your sinful rebellion and self-will, and believe in Jesus as the Savior who takes away all your guilt and sin, making you new. You can pray to Him right now, confessing your sin and putting your faith in His saving work! Instead of remaining in a world of darkness, God offers you sight. You can carry the hope of eternal life and live out that hope now.

Day 23

Father, help me to live with a hope that displays my faith in You, made possible through Your Son, Jesus.

– Reflect –

Read Titus 3:4–7.

1. What led you to place your faith in God's mercy through Jesus? If you have not done this yet, with whom could you speak about taking that step?

2. How do you express your hope in Jesus so that others see your faith?

About the Author

Kevin Freeman has served at Redland for over fifteen years. He and his wife, Karen, have six kids, four of whom came through adoption during Kevin and Karen's time as foster parents. When Kevin is not enjoying ministry at church, he can usually be found spending time with his family, cooking, gardening, or working on a writing project.

– DAY 24 –

Find Unity with Others Through God's Salvation

"For through him we both have access to the Father by one Spirit." (Ephesians 2:18)

I remember when I felt God's presence most profoundly. Recently, our youth ministry went on a mission trip to the Appalachian Mountains. We had just gotten back to the tiny host church where we were staying, and we were tired and drained—both emotionally and physically. We had been pouring into strangers and each other for days on end, and we were reaching the end of our energy.

That night, one of our amazing hosts suggested we wash each other's feet. If you know anything about Gen Z, you know that we do not like feet. And at that point, we preferred just to go to sleep. The idea of washing feet made us feel vulnerable and awkward. It seemed entirely unnecessary, but we did it anyway.

While we embraced discomfort and showed each other a part of ourselves that we were not necessarily proud of, God moved. I remember initially thinking, *Why this? Could we do something—anything—else?* Maybe that was the point! Before any of us realized it, we were on the floor, overwhelmed by the presence of God. We prayed for what felt like forever, words flowing from us, expressing real and deep needs as God revealed them. I remember the sense that God was working among us as words like *revival, miracles, truth, hope, radical love,* and *unity* were spoken. In that moment, God's promises seemed more tangible than ever before. God created us to resonate with special moments like that. How blessed we are to have had the opportunity to feel such deep unity and passion!

The blessing of Christian community is potent, beautiful, and life-changing. It is a much-needed antidote to the isolated, divisive world social media has created. In Ephesians, Paul reminds believers of the amazing benefits offered through Jesus Christ, benefits given to all who trust in Him—no matter their background or their ability to perceive His work in their lives. When I cannot sense God's presence, I go to my friends. They remind me of His goodness and faithfulness in my life. We lift each other up, share each other's burdens, and help each other grow in obedience and holiness. How great a gift is that?

Lord, help me to engage with each person in my life whom You are calling me to pray for or with, and give me the courage and discernment to meet those people where they are and lead them to You.

– Reflect –

Read Ephesians 2:13–22.

1. What holds you back from loving others the way God does?
2. Who in your life needs prayer right now, and how can you pray for them?

About the Author

Grace McGraw grew up attending a different church but fell in love with Redland's youth group when she was in sixth grade. Since then, Grace has been involved in Redland through choir, Vacation Bible School, and an internship. She enjoys music, writing, and learning different languages. Her favorite Bible verse is Psalm 27:13.

– DAY 25 –

Live for the God Who Has Saved You

"And he died for all, that those who live should no longer live for themselves but for him who died for them and was raised again."
(2 Corinthians 5:15)

When I was a little girl, we poked fun at my dad's poor memory. Once, at a birthday party for one of my brothers, he said a prayer and mentioned the wrong child's name! (In fairness, he had five children.) On another occasion, during a church service, he wanted to sing a certain song from the pulpit. But he had to call out to my mother and ask for help remembering the name of the song.

Now I find that I am the one who is frequently forgetful. I may take a long time trying to recall a specific memory, name, or thought that has eluded me. I once heard a psychologist say that it is a good habit to remind ourselves of places and names because this helps maintain memory flow. For example, I can practice memorizing the names of people I need to pray for or the names of new people I have just met. These are habits I can form to help keep my memory sharp.

My spiritual walk also involves habits to help me remember. Specifically, these habits help me remember who I am in Christ. Having devotionals, talking with God, and reading the Bible all remind me of God's goodness toward me. In truth, we are all often forgetful. We are consumed with the failures of our past or are filled with anxiety and guilt that prevent us from recalling and appreciating God's love for us. We need God's Word to remind us who we are and what we are called to do.

Today's passage recalls a glorious truth: Jesus died for us so that we can become new creations in Him. Our Redeemer lives, and He has rescued us from all sin! Incredibly, the one who reconciled us to God has now entrusted to us the ministry of reconciliation, which involves evangelism, sharing the good news of Jesus Christ.

As a new creation in Christ, we daily represent Him as ambassadors. This helps us remember His work in our lives. May our walk, our talk, our smiles, and our generosity reflect a clear testimony of God's love for us. May we also find opportunities to tell others that they too can find life in Jesus.

Dear God, help me remember that I am called to be a witness of Your great love for humanity. Empower me to share this good news with others.

– Reflect –

Read 2 Corinthians 5:14–21.

1. What habits help you remember that you are a new creation in Christ?
2. How do you represent the hope you have in Jesus to those around you?

About the Author

Ruth Figueroa joined Redland when her kids were in school. She was blessed to see her kids develop their faith in Sunday school and youth activities at Redland, and she decided to be baptized at the church. Ruth enjoys the women's ministry and loves the many creative ways Redland reaches the community. Involvement with believers at Redland has helped Ruth grow in her faith and love for Jesus.

God Empowers

– DAY 26 –

Multiply God's Gracious Gifts to Others

"Each of you should give what you have decided in your heart to give, not reluctantly or under compulsion, for God loves a cheerful giver. And God is able to bless you abundantly, so that in all things at all times, having all that you need, you will abound in every good work."
(2 Corinthians 9:7–8)

Have you ever withheld time or resources that you could have given?

Every year, Samaritan's Purse, through its program called Operation Christmas Child, collects shoeboxes filled with gifts to give to children in need around the world. Samaritan's Purse partners with families and churches throughout the United States to donate these boxes, and all the boxes are delivered with the message of the gospel.

My family and I fill a shoebox each year to send to Operation Christmas Child. One year, however, we picked up an empty shoebox and then neglected to fill it. The box sat in our house, visible but ultimately forgotten, because we felt we were too busy to take the time to fill it. We kept putting off the shoebox project and eventually learned that the deadline to turn in filled boxes had passed. We had lost the opportunity.

God calls us to take advantage of opportunities to give to others. We can be generous with our time, money, and other resources. No matter what we give, today's passage highlights what matters most: the posture of our heart. God wants us to give cheerfully, not begrudgingly.

God is the ultimate Giver. He supplies material blessings, and He provides us with the ability to abound in good works, as our passage mentions. The picture Paul presents is of people whose needs have been met by God and are thus enabled to pour their energies into things that have eternal value. And for those who embrace generosity toward the Lord and His Kingdom, an abundant harvest of righteousness awaits.

Nehemiah exemplified a generous spirit. While in exile, he had risen to a position of prestige, trust, and influence as the royal cupbearer to King Artaxerxes. Upon learning the plight of the Israelites in the demolished city of Jerusalem, Nehemiah used his influence on the behalf of God's people. While with them, he continually gave of himself and sacrificed his own energy and safety for their sake. Nehemiah's generous action through his position brought stability to Israel as its walls were rebuilt.

Generosity yields other blessings, too. It encourages thankfulness to God and unity among believers. The apostle Paul penned the words of

2 Corinthians as he was taking up a collection on behalf of Christians facing a famine. Imagine the joy of those believers when they saw their loving, heavenly Father meet their needs through the love and sacrifice of other Christians.

Even if you do not think you have much to offer, there is always something you can do with the resources God has blessed you with. Look for opportunities to share the gifts God has given you. Your generosity may start in small actions, but it will reflect a heart that trusts God to meet your needs and multiply your gifts. Do not miss an opportunity to be a cheerful giver.

Lord, please help me to remember to use Your blessings in my life to serve the church and the community around me.

– Reflect –

Read 2 Corinthians 9:6–16.

1. What needs around you provide an opportunity for you to be generous and to demonstrate your gratitude for the gifts God has given you?

2. How can you spread the gospel through generosity?

About the Author

Edem Setse is fifteen and has lived in Maryland for most of his life. He attends Redland Baptist Church and is a student at Montgomery Blair High School. He likes to code, play video games, and compete in soccer and basketball. He is also very involved in Redland's youth ministry and enjoys opportunities to volunteer at Redland.

– DAY 27 –

Express God's Grace for His Glory

"Each of you should use whatever gift you have received to serve others, as faithful stewards of God's grace in its various forms." (1 Peter 4:10)

At my job, I have been involved in several building renovations, as our workspace uses have changed. During my most recent project, I needed an outlet changed to take a specific plug for a new instrument. I sent pictures of the plug and the paperwork that specified the outlet needed, so I thought we were all on the same page. But when I looked at the outlet that had arrived to be installed, I knew it was not going to fit the plug.

In that moment, my immediate reaction was to rant and blame; I had done my part to make sure the outlet was right, but it was still messed up. And the installation was scheduled for the next day. Rather than reacting emotionally, I took a deep breath and prayed. Then I attempted to stay calm as I pointed out the error to my team, hoping that it could be corrected quickly.

I am so thankful I remained calm. The electrician and I were able to find a solution using parts he had on hand. The outcome was a little less neat but still good. Later, the project manager specifically came by to thank me. Apparently, calm is not the normal response when these sorts of bumps arise, as most people react the way I initially wanted to. The grace that I extended stood out to my colleagues in ways I would not have expected.

In our culture, people are often out to serve themselves first at the expense of others. God calls us to do just the opposite, putting others first and responding like Jesus. He has given each of us gifts and talents that He wants us to use to serve those around us. Our individual combinations of gifts and abilities are all unique, which means we also need one another. We should equally use our gifts and appreciate when others have used theirs, recognizing that these gifts are from God.

God's gifts to us also include the intangible treasures of mercy, grace, and love that He extends to us because He loves us. If God shows us mercy and grace, how can we not do the same to others? Those acts of mercy, grace, and love stand out in our culture, and they can cause people to ask us why we have hope and show grace. This gives us a chance to point to the mercy and grace we have received from God in Christ Jesus. Ultimately, that is what our lives are for, reflecting God's love so that a hurting world sees Him at work.

If our gifts used in service and our small acts of grace can point people to Jesus, why would we not want to share them with everyone?

Day 27

Father God, please let me shine for You in a hurting world and use the gifts You have given me for Your glory. May I disappear in the brightness of You.

– Reflect –

Read 1 Peter 4:7–11.

1. How is the Holy Spirit calling you to serve the people around you?
2. In what ways can you extend God's grace in your normal day?

About the Author

Lisa Jenkins and her husband, Matt, have been members at Redland since they moved from Atlanta in 2005. The amazing people at Redland drew them both in, and they are thankful to call them family. Lisa teaches the three- and four-year-old Sunday school class and leads the women's Tuesday night Bible study.

– DAY 28 –

Act in God's Power, Not in Fear

"For the Spirit God gave us does not make us timid, but gives us power, love and self-discipline." (2 Timothy 1:7)

Have you ever been ashamed? No, I am not talking about the time when you or a loved one did something highly embarrassing, that big slipup when others laughed or jeered at you. And I do not mean that particular sin you now timidly recall with deep regrets—not even that.

Rather, my question is this: Have you ever been ashamed to be a follower of Christ? Or worse yet, have you shrunk back into worldliness after a long, tiring fight against compromise because you felt the pressure of our post-Christian American society? Perhaps you do not even feel ashamed anymore, but instead you feel just a bit numb. Is this the "spirit" you have been given?

In today's Scripture passage, we find the apostle Paul, a voluntary, unashamed slave to Christ. He was a man who had relinquished his freedom to serve the churches, yet he was in chains in a Roman prison (Romans 1:16; 1 Corinthians 9:19; 2 Timothy 2:15). Paul was writing to Timothy, the young pastor in Ephesus, who was feeling timid and was in desperate need of encouragement. Maybe you feel the same way as you read this. I must ask again: Is this the spirit that we should have, either as individual believers or as a church?

Paul exhorts us not to be ashamed of nor timid about the gospel of Jesus Christ, who was crucified and raised from the dead. We are the adopted children of an omnipotent God, mighty in power (Romans 8:15). Our God is

> the LORD, the LORD, the compassionate and gracious God, slow to anger, abounding in love and faithfulness, maintaining love to thousands, and forgiving wickedness, rebellion and sin. Yet he does not leave the guilty unpunished. (Exodus 34:6–7)

He created the universe from nothing (Genesis 1:1). He brought Israel out of Egypt with a mighty hand and an outstretched arm, with great terror and with signs and wonders (Deuteronomy 26:8). He condescended to be born as a human baby in order to save us from our sin, and, by His death and Resurrection, He has given us a living hope (Romans 5:1–5). We are His children (1 John 3:1)! Therefore, the encouragement God gave to Joshua can be ours as well: "Be strong and courageous. Do not be afraid; do not be discouraged, for the LORD your God will be with you wherever you go" (Joshua 1:9).

Day 28

Lord, You are sovereign. You are mighty. You can do all things; no purpose of Yours can be thwarted. Embolden me to speak and act in truth with love today.

– Reflect –

Read 2 Timothy 1:6–11.

1. What kind of spirit should we have, both individually and as a church (universal and local)?

2. Knowing that Paul and other believers throughout the centuries have suffered for the sake of the gospel, how strong is your resolve to remain steadfast in your devotion to Christ?

About the Author

Collin Lobb is a devoted Christian, Redland member, loving husband, and father of three beautiful girls.

– DAY 29 –

Trade Bondage for Freedom

"For those who are led by the Spirit of God are the children of God." (Romans 8:14)

One night, my wife, Heidi, and I watched the movie *Walt Before Mickey*, which tells the story of Walt Disney before he created the iconic character Mickey Mouse. Disney led a hard life. His father doubted him, his first business failed, and the employees in his second business left because their paychecks were bouncing. Heidi commented, "It is good that we know the end." Knowing the later success that Disney would enjoy made the movie easier for us to watch, but Walt Disney himself knew no guarantee of later success.

Our lives are similar. We often wish that we could know what will happen in the future. But in fact, because of the work of Jesus, we do know the end. We know that Jesus is preparing a place for us and that He will make us holy through the work of the Holy Spirit. In the short term, we are sometimes tempted to give up, but knowing our future hope enables us to endure.

Some in our society would argue that our lives are predetermined by our genes, our social status, or our family background; they believe we are who we are because we are born that way. But as children of God, we are not trapped in the patterns and identity of our former lives; instead, we are empowered toward transformation through the Holy Spirit. I once was stingy, but now I enjoy giving generously to the church. I once thought that all love was self-serving, but I have since experienced sacrificial love. I once saw no sense in prayer, but now I pray regularly.

My mother had some obsessive-compulsive traits; for example, if she did not put her shoes on in the right order, she had doubts about how the rest of the day would proceed. I might have some of the same anxious tendencies, but when I feel tempted to fret over such things, I remind myself of the words of the famous hymn: "On Christ, the solid Rock, I stand: all other ground is sinking sand."[2] I will put my faith in God, rather than in the order in which I put on my shoes.

Christians are given certainty about the future to come, as well as hope for the here and now. With God's Spirit dwelling in us, we can walk in righteousness and live in freedom because we have the certain hope of an eternity with our Savior and Lord.

Father, help me to remember that I am Your child, and give me the power to live as I should.

– Reflect –

Read Romans 8:9–15.

1. When do you feel the most stuck and unable to change?
2. How can the knowledge of your freedom as God's child help you face today's challenges?

About the Author

Brad Chaney is a former atheist who came to faith in Christ after examining the evidence of Christ's Resurrection from the dead. Professionally, he is a political scientist who conducts research on public policy. He and Heidi are both members at Redland, where Brad serves as a deacon and a teacher.

– DAY 30 –

Wear Holiness Through God's Love

"Therefore, as God's chosen people, holy and dearly loved, clothe yourselves with compassion, kindness, humility, gentleness and patience." (Colossians 3:12)

Many years ago, shortly before we were to take our daughter back to college for her sophomore year, I stuck my head in her bedroom door to check on the progress of her packing. She had her clothes carefully folded and arranged in little piles all over the floor; it was as if her drawers and wardrobe had somehow exploded in an orderly fashion. A closer look at her various stacks revealed that she was packing according to certain outfits. I asked her about that, and she confirmed my assumption. She explained her process:

- There were piles of outfits she had set aside that were appropriate for morning classes and others for afternoon classes.
- There was clothing selected that would be suitable for just hanging around the dorm.
- There were dresses and skirts to wear to worship on Sundays.

- She had selected a few outfits that would be appropriate for the fall season up in Pennsylvania, when the weather begins to turn cold.
- She had even packed three bags of a wide variety of footwear to compliment her clothing.

If you have daughters, you are familiar with this kind of wardrobe prep. Our girls tend to take clothing very seriously!

There is a sense in which all Christians should feel the same way about what they "wear"—because God repeatedly tells us in His Word the kinds of "clothing" His children should put on:

- Ephesians 4:22, 24 says to "put off your old self, which is being corrupted by its deceitful desires" and to "put on the new self, created to be like God in true righteousness and holiness."
- Romans 13:14 says, "Rather, clothe yourselves with the Lord Jesus Christ, and do not think about how to gratify the desires of the flesh."
- 1 Peter 5:5 says, "All of you, clothe yourselves with humility toward one another, because, 'God opposes the proud but shows favor to the humble.'"
- And today's reading says, "Therefore, as God's chosen people, holy and dearly loved, clothe yourselves with compassion, kindness, humility, gentleness, and patience."

Jerry Bridges refers to the attitudes or virtues in "God's dress code" as "garments of grace."[3] I love this phrase because these various "garments" are indeed undeserved gifts of God—precious attributes that help us to stand out as His children. We each must ask God to nurture the growth of these attributes in our lives because we cannot experience abundant life without them. Unless we "dress" this way, we cannot be effective and fruitful disciples.

And we *do* need God's help with this. We cannot be truly virtuous on our own. This is what Jesus was getting at in John 15:5, when He said, "If you remain in me and I in you, you will bear much fruit; apart from me you can do nothing."

Paul also refers to this principle at the end of today's reading, when he says, "And whatever you do, whether in word or deed, do it all in the name of [and in the *strength* of] the Lord Jesus, giving thanks to God the Father through him" (Colossians 3:17).

Father God, help me to clothe myself every day in ways that show I am Your child.

– Reflect –

Read Colossians 3:12–17.

1. Of the "clothing items" mentioned (kindness, compassion, gentleness, humility, patience), which do you most need to put on?

2. What attitudes in your "wardrobe" do you need to "put off" or throw away?

About the Author

In 2023, Mark Adams retired from fifty years of ministering to and with God's people. The years he is most thankful for are the ones (all thirty-three of them!) that he used to serve the people of Redland Baptist Church. These days, Mark enjoys time with his grandkids and serves churches in Montgomery County through pulpit supply or as an interim pastor. Mark says, "I am privileged to hold the title of pastor emeritus at Redland Baptist Church."

Next Steps

Thank you for taking the time to read the devotionals in this book. Our hope is that you were encouraged, refreshed, and drawn closer to Christ as you engaged with each devotional.

So, what is next?

If you already have a church home or live outside the DC area, we are thankful for an opportunity to be a blessing in your life. May God continue to bless you and your church.

If you happen to live in our area and do not currently have a church home, we would love to connect with you. Come join us for a worship service or spend time in Bible study with some of our devotional authors. No matter where you are in your spiritual journey, you are welcome to follow Jesus along with us.

At Redland, we aim to help people connect with the heart of Christ. We would love to help you make that connection as you pursue a deeper relationship with Him.

Every Sunday, we conclude our worship service with the following benediction (or "blessing") that is based on Colossians 3:15–17. These are fitting words to conclude this devotional book:

> Let the peace of Christ rule in your hearts, since as members of one body, you are called to peace. Let the word of Christ dwell in you richly, and this week, whatever you

> do in word or in deed, do it all in the name of Christ, giving thanks to God the Father through Him.

This is our prayer for you, dear reader!

Sincerely,
Redland Baptist Church

Endnotes

1. Karya Naz Balkiz, "Eşref Armağan: A Blind Turkish Painter Who Sees Through His Fingertips," Turkish Radio and Television World, accessed October 9, 2024, https://www.trtworld.com/magazine/esref-armagan-a-blind-turkish-painter-who-sees-through-his-fingertips-12770321.

2. Edward Mote, "My Hope Is Built on Nothing Less," 1834, Hymnary.org, https://hymnary.org/text/my_hope_is_built_on_nothing_less.

3. Jerry Bridges, "Garments of Grace," in *Transforming Grace: Living Confidently in God's Unfailing Love* (NavPress, 1991), 195.

Made in the USA
Middletown, DE
23 January 2025

69424770R00092